NORTH

AMERICAN

STADIUMS

NORTH AMERICAN STADIUMS

poems

Grady Chambers

MILKWEED EDITIONS

First paperback edition, published 2021 by Milkweed Editions
Printed in Canada
Cover design by Mary Austin Speaker with vector images by love pattern / Shutterstock
Author photo by Jessica Scicchitano
21 22 23 24 25   5 4 3 2 1
First Paperback Edition

978-1-57131-535-9
Milkweed Editions, an independent nonprofit publisher, gratefully acknowledges sustaining support from our Board of Directors; the Alan B. Slifka Foundation and its president, Riva Ariella Ritvo-Slifka; the Amazon Literary Partnership; the Ballard Spahr Foundation; *Copper Nickel*; the McKnight Foundation; the National Endowment for the Arts; the National Poetry Series; the Target Foundation; and other generous contributions from foundations, corporations, and individuals. Also, this activity is made possible by the voters of Minnesota through a Minnesota State Arts Board Operating Support grant, thanks to a legislative appropriation from the arts and cultural heritage fund. For a full listing of Milkweed Editions supporters, please visit milkweed.org.

Library of Congress Cataloging-in-Publication Data

Names: Chambers, Grady, author.
Title: North American stadiums : poems / Grady Chambers.
Description: First edition. | Minneapolis : Milkweed Editions, [2020] |
    Summary: "Winner of the inaugural Max Ritvo Poetry Prize, selected by
    Henri Cole"-- Provided by publisher.
Identifiers: LCCN 2020010539 (print) | LCCN 2020010540 (ebook) | ISBN
    9781571315359 (paperback) | ISBN 9781571319937 (ebook)
Subjects: LCGFT: Poetry.
Classification: LCC PS3603.H354 N67 2020 (print) | LCC PS3603.H354
    (ebook) | DDC 811/.6--dc23
LC record available at https://lccn.loc.gov/2020010539
LC ebook record available at https://lccn.loc.gov/2020010540

Milkweed Editions is committed to ecological stewardship. We strive to align our book production practices with this principle, and to reduce the impact of our operations in the environment. We are a member of the Green Press Initiative, a nonprofit coalition of publishers, manufacturers, and authors working to protect the world's endangered forests and conserve natural resources. *North American Stadiums* was printed on acid-free 100% postconsumer-waste paper by Friesens Corporation.

Contents

Explaining the Resurrection in Simple Words / 1

I

Syracuse, October / 5
The Life / 6
Another Beauty I Remember / 8
Thousand Islands / 11
Sunday Morning / 14
Far Rockaway / 15
Jackknife / 20
A Summer / 26

II

View from Brooklyn / 29
The Window / 30
Pin / 34
Dragons / 38
The Syracuse Poem / 44
Blue Handgun / 49

III

After Psalm 17 / 57
A Story about the Moon / 59
Dispatch: Pittsburgh / 60
Picasso in Milwaukee / 63
Dispatch: Canal Zone / 64

Salt Lake / 67
Forbes Field, Pittsburgh, 1966 / 68

IV

The Leavings / 73
Calaveras / 78
Bands You Might Have Liked If You Were Still Alive / 80
Stopping the War / 82
Rainout in the Twin Cities / 91
Memorial Day / 92

Acknowledgments / 95

NORTH

AMERICAN

STADIUMS

Explaining the Resurrection in Simple Words

A blessing can be the act
of invoking divine
protection,
or a favor or gift
bestowed by god,
and I don't know
how to define mercy,
but the field
is lit like the heart
of the night, gnats flitting
above the crosshatched grass,
huge shadows of the ballplayers in stadium light
whistling in signals
from the outfield.
The wind lifts and settles
our shirts against our skin,
and you ask after my day:
there'd been pinwheels
spinning on a rain-soaked lawn, pigeons
cooing and nesting in the gutters.
I'd pressed my back to the dark
damp wood of the trunk.
Yellow flowers fell on me.

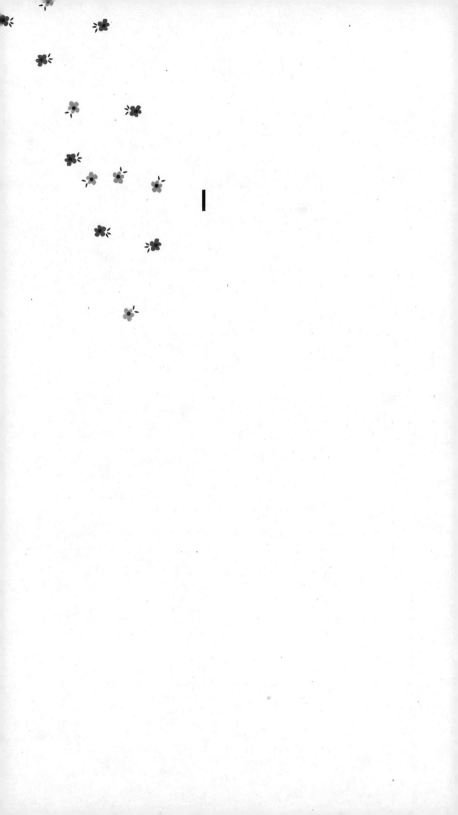

I

Syracuse, October

Fuck the hot autumns of Charleston, fuck handsome
Alabama, fuck the Deep South alcoholics

standing in flannel in the summer sun. I drove north.
I took Green Road to Hubbardsville

and saw October in August, booted men hosing grit
off the park pool's bottom, crisp leaves lifted

like the remnants of summer's collective memory.
I drove out or into it listening to the Liverpool Choir's

mournful version of the national anthem, the tuning forks
of eastern townships bringing a Stravinsky more film score

than symphony. I wanted the blaze of the unmuffled
trumpet, the spin song of the laundromat, a little of the
        hurricane's

Guernican remedy in the streeted leaves, in the blooms
of glass from kids breaking fluorescent

light tubes in the spent vocabulary
of an asphalt parking lot. I wanted

October: lace trim of a black dress slumped
on the floor of my birthday, cold skin

and laughter. Little burn on the leaves, little love
declaration; little dull light in the white sky.

The Life

So I drove while she nosed the folds of my sweatshirt
on the bench seat of the Chevy and fell in love

with my smell of ice rinks and rubber though my heart belonged
to other beloveds: stanchions of high-voltage lines

and the stalled horizon or something
as simple as a sparse line of gulls

gliding over the winter lake.
My personal philosophy's a second-story porch: bee-eaten

beams, wobbly and rotted, corners filled
with the day's leavings: I liked Bach

for a time and she my soft hands and I
her sun-bleached Cleveland beginnings: but the sepia pictures

and not the life, how their color reminded me of old
photos of ballplayers from the early twentieth century,

and I liked more the skateboarder
clearing leaves from the avenue's cluttered gutters

and the street psychic stating the obvious: it's November
and we could all use some luck. So we hit Milwaukee

and why? Why not: the art museum was startling,
church wood and folk art and the cracked expanse

of lake ice through the windows. So she liked my mind
or kind eyelashes and bulldozed my back as I fumbled

to say something pretty to bridge the distance.
And we bowled in a basement alley; and we got loaded

and sober and saw the wind carry a leaf
like a hand, stem down, brown palm open

and twirling like a waiter carrying a tray
brimming with champagne flutes: it would take us to

Detroit, Chicago, the spread Midwest, the sun setting
where it always does, Iowa

before winter's end: where we felt the cold come down
through the hours to a moment fluttered open

like a shuffled deck: taillights on the highway
in patterned brigade, smoke bolstered through idling pipes;

her wondering who I loved, the horseshoe shadow
of my arms proclaiming *this, all this.*

Another Beauty I Remember

Somewhere in South Chicago the millwrights and welders
of US Steel are leaving their masks
to hooks and lockers and shining out
into evening still covered in dust.
Those men do not belong to me, their world of arc
and fire, but many nights I have loved them.

*

When I was seventeen
my friends and I rode each weekend
toward the Indiana border. One drove, another worked the dials
on the radio, and I drank gin in the back
and ordered us to slow over the toll bridge
to peer down at the barge lights roaming the Calumet River,
then up to where the smokestacks of US Steel
rose like an organ in a church. Gin, fire, the workers
coming off their shifts, light lighting up the metal-dust
spread along their shoulders like the men
had all walked through plate glass windows.

*

Their dust does not belong to me, but many nights I have loved them.
They do not live where I was born, north of the mammoth
glass residences of the Gold Coast
where the worst news
was soon mended: a neighbor girl's bone
broken in a fall. A garage fire sullying the air
over Broadway and Balmoral. I did not know
their sons: the Byrnes, the Walshes, the Mansekies
of Bridgeport and Fuller Park. The green parade and the green

river and the pride of the Irish. Laughter, bright
balloons over cracked asphalt, yellow hair
and sunlight, all the families singing songs
of another country.

*

I keep taking the long road back
to that summer because the image won't leave me:
weekend evenings, gin and driving south, smoke
blasting from the factory stacks,
the men glancing up at the flash of our passing.
We were going to spend all night drinking gin
on an Indiana beach. Dust had settled
like fragments of a hand grenade, like silver wings
across the backs of the men. We were going to tell each other
what was beautiful.

*

The dark water was beautiful. The fire drowning
the air with smoke, our voices
drowned by the sound.
I stood at the edge of the water
where the coastline stretched from my left
and curved enough north that the stitch
of factory lights looked like they were shining
from the far side of the lake.
We burned traces into the air with the burning
tips of sticks poked into the heart of fire.
We all said the sky was beautiful. Our bodies light
against the water.

*

Somewhere in South Chicago the millwrights and welders
of US Steel are leaving their masks to hooks
and they are going home. What did I know then? What did I know
of the beauty of the men?
Driving past, I watched just long enough
to see them stepping out of their shifts,
believing them angelic, knowing not a thing
about their lives, each of them, perhaps, seeing what I saw: light
coming off the backs of the others as they drifted
into the lot, but knowing the light I saw was dust,
not wings, and, knowing to call it dust,
calling it dust.

Thousand Islands

Just past border patrol we round the corner
toward Thousand Islands Bridge
when the car coming toward us veers and Kira cries out
and braces against the sweep of headlights
as the car nears and straightens and skids
then straightens and in a spit of snow
comes to rest on the shoulder, quiet,
undamaged, ticking. I'm as nervous as Kira
though I try not to show it as she sighs
back into her seat.

After Michael died, Mark went to rehab
and Danny lost his hair and disappeared
each weekend into the High Sierra,
and Brian worked his torso into a perfect board, a stacked
    abdomen
and a thick grid of veins raised beneath his forearms
when he flexed.
After Michael died, we stood in a basement
and drank soda out of plastic cups and watched a montage
of him becoming young again.

We reach the peak of the bridge
and Kira leans to the window to watch the bricked ice
glide by below, and what I remember is
we flew a kite, Michael and I, a grey November Saturday,
he knelt in a field and pulled it from its box,
shimmied the rods into the slits,
the cloth growing taut across the frame.

He threw me the spool and jogged out
and shouted, *Now!* freeing the kite while I reeled in the
   string to make it climb.
And it did, it lifted, he whooped and stumbled toward me,
he took the spool from my hands and zigzagged out
across the darkening field, his eyes skyward, his tongue
   curled
from the corner of his mouth, Michael, Gordo, chubby
in his Little League tee, undone buttons, his chest
a soft shelf of flesh, his eyes tight in concentration.

And time passed, it grew cold, I slipped my hands
into my sleeves, a dog barked, I called, *Michael, Michael*, he
   shrugged
and chinned the air, *Look at it!* It made a ragged snap,
it seemed proud, what color was it? It hung there like a wish,
   I said,
Michael, pleading, I wanted to go home.

I tell none of this to Kira as the wipers rise and fall
against the snow.
How could I explain it? My friends
working their bodies into youth
as they grow older, Michael tethered to a kite
while I called his name,
the snowy road, night falling.

And how can I explain that when she puffs her bottom lip
and blows her bangs from her eyes
there is so much love inside me
I want to pull the car to the shoulder
and hold her there, while all I can do

is nod at the shoreline
and say, *When it's warm, we'll come back here.*

And I think that maybe we will—a weekend in a cabin,
a stone path sloping down to water, the river
in front of her, her hands shading her forehead—

and she just turns the heat up and smiles, and I accelerate
down the last drop of the bridge,
and our stomachs jump into our throats, and we coast
back into the country where we were born.

Sunday Morning

The weather turned bad and I got happy.
That's wrong—I mean the morning sky

was ash blue, birds on the ground. I mean
not happy but good, not good

but fastened, steady, like every train in the city
was running late, but no one minded.

On 12th Street, tarpaulin swelled
and bowed in wind. Rain drove straight

through a woman's dress. And again
on Hollis, that slowness: damp black

trees, the line of streetlights
paced like breath. I pulled over. Leaves

dripped like rinsed hands.
A girl held her mother

.by the shoulders on a porch.

Far Rockaway

Not this one
says the woman on the platform
this one
is going to Lefferts
you want the next one
the one to Far Rockaway
and I nod
though I've never been there
it is the train I am waiting for
though it's cold
as I picture it
white dunes
Far Rockaway
waves
with grey hair

I remember that movie
where the actor known for comedy
wears a black jacket
is melancholy
in winter skips work
and rides the train past blackbirds
all day
far boroughs
and his own reflection

what awaits him
is a beach in winter
gulls and stone
in one scene

he just stands there
spinning
in another
a stranger
peeks her head
above the train seat
they hate each other
sporadically
share a cigarette
and fall in love

I was sixteen and my heart hurt
to watch it
it made me want to be older
and lonesome
handsome
with brown hair
and an empty pier
a winter
where I could be alone

that year I read *A Coney Island
of the Mind* met Genevieve
mimicked my body
with pillows stuffed beneath my sheets
sneaking out to the lake
beneath a pink
winter sky
silver flask of vodka
the freezing water
heaving like a sea

that actor
the last I heard
stopped being funny
grew a beard
voted
fell in love
with a woman
thin as a wing
who OD'd
a quiet suicide
of white pills

for two winters
I read Genevieve
Ferlinghetti
we drank together
through the dark afternoons
Far Rockaway we said
and meant something pretty
something very far away
Far Rockaway
against the poverty of suitcases
Far Rockaway
like an optimism
on Sunday afternoon
Far Rockaway for the thing we made
and didn't want
and lost in an airport bathroom
spilled out
in a black clump of blood

before the train comes
the rush of air
people on the platform standing
a kid pulls at his sister
a man rests his hand on his suitcase
like it's the head of a child

I was born in Chicago
I live in Los Angeles
Ferlinghetti is alive
in San Francisco
Genevieve too
though I don't know where
Far Rockaway
like a prayer
all those years
I was scared for her
she nearly drank herself to death

so many lives
seem possible
so many Rockaways
a beach in a movie
    snow stacked on sand
or a place where the dead go
    stiff bodies stanchioned
like foundations for a pier

you could walk between them
she once said
touch them

if you wanted
their eyes frozen open
toward the shore

light bends where the tracks curve
around the billboards
four grey birds scared into air
I am old as the actor was
when I first watched him
walk the white beach
I thought was Far Rockaway
though I still don't have brown hair
I still remember
I wanted to be older
and lonesome
be handsome
and an empty pier
a winter
as the train comes
where I could be alone
but everyone I love could reach me

Jackknife

If I said red-
    handled jack-
knife blade.

If I played for you
    a grainy recording
of a switcher's whistle
moaning
in the distance.
    If I pointed

to the post road, the woods beyond it,
Brockton, November
eating all
the light,
would you remember?

We are kneeling
in the leaves, Jacob.
I am muddying my knees
beside you.
We are seventeen.
Your mother's death
between us
like a stone.

*

I am muddying my knees
beside you—
I am watching you work

the knife beneath the scruff
 of the bark,
and I am still
in love: your corded
   forearms swollen
in the cold,
 drained hands
peeling clean the branch—

the swayback

blade, Jacob, the sky
and the wind, the slip
that opened up an inch of skin
like a butterfly
in the thick
of your palm—

the knife just
 dropped, forgotten
where it landed.

*

Twenty-eight years
and what have I given you?
A knee to the eye.
A throat-hold
on a schoolyard court,
our knees gashed by asphalt.
So violence,
Jacob, but tenderness
too—fingers on the neck
of the other, stigmata

of a split
sclera, a whole boyhood
of putting stitches to each other
like time-marks
knifed into a wall.

*

In my dreams
I see her. Whole generations
are gathering
on the front porch
for a picture. She is walking
through my childhood
lawn. She is walking past
the fence,
unimpressed.
She is admonishing me
for the mud
still dripping
from my sneakers,
the dirt at my hemline,
my insufficient hands.
I've never told you.
And she is whole again.

*

We are fourteen.
We are learning geometry.
We are learning the words
to the Declaration, how to count in Latin.
We are reading *On the Road*
to each other like a Bible,
naming the chambers

of a reptile heart, how the shapes
of flame can change
depending what they burn around.
Toothpick bridges. Your mother's illness born
in the shift of a cell. A night sky
made from a trash-bag
tent. Lying beside you
in the darkness.

*

I'm sorry. Electronic
    pulse. Intercom echo
even in the stairwells. Twenty-seven steps.
    The bar-handle
of the metal door. When I saw the knot
    of tubes I thought
of a highway. Her chest swollen
    like a sodden log
bobbing in the water.

*

The night you heard
I didn't answer.
I never told you.
The telephone crying
like a gate alarm.
I never told you.
How silence
slides through years.
I've never told you.
The little hole
that opens
when I speak—

*

Weight
on the balls of your feet.
   Sneaker toe box crushed

in your crouch, the inch of air
      between your heels

and the forest floor—

tongue and laces,
   Jacob, the sky

in the blade, the slip, the blade
   in your hand, your breath

suddenly full of knuckles.

*

If you are running.
If you are clutching the torn
T-shirt tourniquet rigged
around your hand.
If I can fix it.
If I am slowing.
If I am turning back
to the forest, tracing
the snapped
branches back, stepping back
again into the beds
our footprints pressed
into the earth.
If I can find

the peeled branches.
If the blade
is still beside them.
If I fold it back to its hold.
If I lay the blade back
in your hand,
if I place it—

A Summer

In June my dog died. By the sex shop on Belmont, a guy carried a sign with *Last Days* printed in fat black letters, and he could be forgiven for thinking so: the city was steaming; commuters shook open their papers; capitalism seemed to collapse, then didn't; men howled from their jail cells all across the South. I wanted to feel real grief, and did, the way my mother lifted the dead dog off the vet's metal slab, then held it to her chest as if it were a child, and merely sleeping. But driving home, she showed me the first house she lived in with my father. That night we cried, lit a candle, drank cold white wine on the dark back porch. What I mean is it felt good to sit there; it felt like I could feel time open outward like a swimmer opens water: in July, an ex-girlfriend called about a jacket she'd never given back. We made plans. By August I'd forgotten the sign but remembered the man standing under the flat sky, diminished, the grey traffic passing behind him. The heat broke; August kept on going. I drove my mother to the shore, scattered the dog's ashes, dove in.

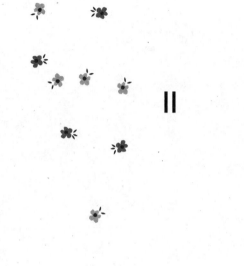

II

View from Brooklyn

The city was inside the water. The sun was there too, pierced
by a spire. A helicopter flew through glass.
Standing on the Promenade, I took a picture of it,
stepped back, took another of the people
taking pictures of people posed against the real city rising
on the river's other side. I was reminded in the way
the people were arrayed of a picture I love and cut
from a spread depicting the crowd at Canaveral
standing beneath a moonshot Apollo, everyone—
the sun behind them—
made into shadow. There was a shine
to my picture. There was a shrine down the walkway,
a broken wreath, some torn strings
tied to the fence. I took a picture of the votives,
the buildings in the river. *Where were you*
and you instantly remember.

The Window

This was my routine: I woke, and in the morning
carried my houseplants to the courtyard,
three small succulents
potted in a wooden box.
Each evening I returned to retrieve them.

When a neighbor inquired,
I explained that I did this to give the plants sun and air.
Her manner suggested she perceived my action to be
unusual—I suspected she'd been watching for some time.

Soon after, the rains came.
What little light there was
only made visible the water
that had been falling invisibly all night.
The daily journey from the kitchen to the courtyard became
    unnecessary.

Here I should explain something
about the room in which I lived.
It was small, three walls and a door,
but one whole wall was a window.
The view was of the courtyard
and across it, windows into the rooms
on the yard's far side: blinds, reflections,
individual panes the width and length of coffins.

In time I became interested in a window opposite my own.
It was like the others
in most respects, except all day a curtain

was drawn across it. Light burned
from behind it all hours of the night.

Evenings I positioned my chair behind the blinds—

night came. One by one
the windows glowed
on the building opposite.
One by one they were extinguished
except the one I watched.
I recall a night-light I was given as a boy,
a moon the size of my hand
illuminated by a slim bulb.

The light shined through the moon; the moon's plastic
softened the light.
In the sky, the white moon.
In the corner of my room, the small moon appeared yellow.
    The window
came to seem connected: the way the curtain
held and thickened the light,
how the light made the weight of the curtain apparent.

Reading back, I see that I have omitted
certain important details—

many nights had passed; the curtain remained closed.
What I knew of the room I knew
only from the shadows cast
by the objects inside—

a headboard,
maybe,
a spray of stems.
I never saw anyone.

I never saw anyone,
but I knew the room was occupied: the shade of the light
sometimes altered, bright or dim
depending on the night,
like a pulse.

I lay in bed. The rain erased the world,
then slowed,
and the world's noise returned—
trickling water; the hum
coming from the walls.
Days passed. A stain formed
on the sill's tile around the outline
of the box of plants.

The window, as I have said, often remained lit
late into the night. When I saw it, I would rise
and turn on my own light. If the window darkened,
mine did too. In this way, I felt, we came to form
a kind of correspondence.

At the courtyard's center
sat a round glass table, four white chairs
tilted toward it, like people conspiring.

A pool of water formed across the table's surface,
blue in the evening, pale in the day, the sky
moving inside it. Each night before sleep,
my eyes traveled from the window
to the table, from the table to the shape
of each vacant chair, the darkness filling
the absent forms.

Pin

On my eleventh birthday my sister gave me a pin.
It was small—as light in weight as a charm
on a child's neck—and so thin
as to be indiscernible.

That was the year Mrs. Bergen explained to me
a penny dropped from the tallest building in the city
could split open a sidewalk. My sister had slipped
and snapped her arm falling from the jungle gym
and this was, I suppose,
the teacher's way of trying to comfort me.

It snowed that winter.
I pictured the bone being pulled from her arm
like an arrow from a sheath, a new one
slid into its place. I noticed the new attention
she received at school and tracked it back

to the day she fell: a circle of boys
had huddled over something
on the ground. I'd pushed through
to where she lay, curled up
and covered in wood chips,
like they'd been burying her.
It was in those months that I began to wear the pin.
When I couldn't sleep, I held it
like a talisman. I told it everything
that scared me.

There was a time, of course,
when the events I have just described
were more or less forgotten: the bone healed,
then lengthened. We grew up. She moved
to a different city. Pictures of her life
flashed across my screen: a skyline
seen from a balcony; someone's shadow
overlapping her own. A country road,
a fire pit, a horse, the ocean. She felt far from me,
and was.

Perhaps it is that distance that brought it back,
the day the saw peeled off the cast
like a skin, the new arm emerging
thin and sickly, paler
than the other. It seemed a part of her
that hadn't been there before.

What I can say is that the fixed year between us
seemed to grow. A letter was passed to me
by a high school boy
to give to her. The tank top
we used to share was left folded
on my pillow. My own behavior became

peculiar to me. I crushed a bird
beneath the wheel of my bicycle.
I called my sister over to watch it
drag itself into the garden.

What it was I didn't know, but I saw it
in the flushed soft faces of the girls ascending
from the basement showers

after gym glass, damp stains
where their wet braids had fallen
on their shoulders. I saw it in assembly,
the way Sasha Lavotnick's hand would drift
and trace the outline of the straps
showing through the shirt of the girl beside her.
It was so delicate I understood
a boy would never be allowed
to touch a girl in that way,
and wouldn't think to.

Noon meant recess. On the huge field, drained
by winter, we stood like tribes:
girls circled together with girls;
the boys drew lines for games.
In our corner, a centerfold of a famous actress
passed between our hands. One night, Bobby Richmond
asked me to mimic the woman's position
on the edge of his bed. I lay down;
his mother was asleep.

After, we stood at his window
watching traffic pass
on the road below. We spoke,
I remember, about wanting to be older.

I live now in two small rooms—a kitchen
and a place to sleep. Outside: the yard,
a high blank wall, a small section of sky.
The pin, always fragile,
bent some time ago.
I have made a place for it
on scraps of old fabric

on the stand beside my bed.
I think of a city, my sister disappearing
down the subway steps.
Holding her umbrella, the wind
of the train lifting her hair.

The winter the bone broke
we found a trunk of shawls
in the attic, the fabric thin and worn, almost weightless.
When our mother came to find us,
we sat with our backs turned,
wrapped in the cold dark silks,
pretending we were very old women
who had lived there all along.

She asked our names. We'd forgotten.
Stiff beneath the cloak, in its cast,
my sister's arm looked thick as a statue's.
When our mother asked us
where her children were,
we stifled our laughter.
We said, *You have none.*

Dragons

I was having trouble sleeping.
To try, I drank. When I slept, I sweated, woke
in early darkness, stumbled up to piss.
Back in bed, I remembered things—
a Christmas party I went to as a boy—
the breath of the adults—
the children's hands
taken into bigger hands, our endurance
as our faces were touched, our hair touched, rearranged.

I walked all day to exhaust myself.
Buses were long insects
turning onto Broadway.
In this way the winter passed.

*

But it didn't pass.
I was living in the north,
and the sky was a stone,
blank and frozen.

At night it lightened, pink,
fed by the glow from the town.
By morning it returned,
whiter, lower.

Every twenty-six days I flew south for a weekend with my sister.
Each time I appeared she seemed in some distress—
her brown hair, once thick, was thinning—

the drain was clogged—
and I tended to her before returning.

Back in my rooms, I opened the cabinet.
I closed it.
I thought:

if I could wait till 8:00 p.m.—
if I had a half glass of water in between—

the second and third drink—

the fifth and the sixth.
I lay awake. I thought of distant ships
flinching toward each other
on the green screen of a ship's radar,
a mass at the bottom
to represent land.

*

There was a dragon in the book
my father read to me when I was young.
It flew over cities. Its nails
were claws. Its head was
noble, broad and scaled.

It slept with its face
tucked beneath its wing, in the rear of its cave,
chained.

It was protecting something,
or had been forced to.

Through the wall, my neighbor moaned
in a way I envied—to be so filled.

I got up and poured—
the torches of planes
passed through the sky.

Time passed as slow as a hair
trying to grow through skin.

Snow fell.

Time passed
fast as that same hair
cut by a razor.

*

In February I went south, fixed blinds
to her windows, cleaned her rugs.

She seemed better,
and worse. She slept, but her hair had grown sparser,
the dark strands
stark against her pale scalp.

What ailed her was inexplicable—
I thought of how our dog used to gnaw its tail
till it bled.

I stood by the window
until the windows opposite became slim
lit bars.

She toppled a plate
as I packed to leave.
We circled the date of my next visit.

*

It became important to me
whether the dragon was good.
Who were the women who came to visit it
in their dresses, with their scepters?
What was it guarding?

I couldn't remember—

was the dragon kind? Would it hurt
just to hurt?

Its tail could sweep men
into a moat at a flick.

When it breathed,
something burned—

its whole body seemed a weapon.

*

There was a place between the sixth and eighth drink
where everything diminished,
the body inside but at a distance
from the wall of the shell but
still encased in the thin lucid membrane—

needles, tubes, the soul's liquid
filling up a glass—

she'd called to say they'd drained a cyst—

and I stood in my living room
as I'd once stood as a child
on the shore, in the tide,
the draining sand sinking
my feet deeper, my arms out for balance—

*

At the terminal I arrived at in her city
the moving walkway was always broken.
A display of miniature weather balloons
in festive colors adorned the air
near the ceiling, in all seasons,

and because they were there in all seasons
and because the defining features of my visits
were the ebb and flow of her condition,
and the nights spent by the window watching
light return to other windows
as the day came,

the visits, over time, grew indistinct from one another,
like the trick of the one bright silk
in the clown's fist
becoming many
and then becoming one again.

The balloons appeared to float.

I went back and forth from my sister's door.

We grew close.

She took an interest in my duffel
and when it became worn,
she bought another, and another in anticipation
of that one's deteriorating condition.

Beside them, in the closet, she made a space
for my sweaters.
Frost spread across the windows.

And when I was having trouble sleeping,
to try, I drank.

And when I slept, I sweated, woke
in darkness, stumbled up to piss.

And when I was back in bed
I would remember things—
a Christmas party I attended as a boy—
the breath of the adults—
the sky lowering each morning—
the dragon sleeping over its bars of gold.

The Syracuse Poem

In St. Joseph's locked ward the bedbound wither
like dying lakes
in the West. Late prayers are spoken backward
to the high windows
rising over the prone
rows of bodies: winter leans
on the waste plants—
the creeks freeze; winter feeds
from the paper factory's stacks
like a mouth attached to an exhaust pipe.

*

Who lives there? I don't know
what they dream. Mounds of fresh snow grow
and turn black and cave
back in on themselves.
Where the interstate
splits the city, the buildings
look like chimneys. I look up
at the numbered hives
where the sad and insane
are made invisible. I see dark windows
and think of paint peeling thickly
off the stairwell walls.

*

For seven months I watched a man die
on a park bench
on Trinity—slowly
his skin constricted

toward his bones like a tire
losing air.

All December thick
splashes of blood spilled
from his throat
across the snow.
In spring it dribbled from him
when he breathed.

*

But I was not born here,
and who am I
to speak of its deaths?

        (Wind touches the web so
      the spider swings
          across my window
      like a scythe)

Still, I record it, the naked hook
of the girl's exposed prosthetic
hand attached to the handle
of her bag.

Still, I call it beautiful.

But,
I am not the prosperous Baldwinsville sons
dining behind the glass
on Clinton Street;
I am not the mother
in the bleachers

cheering for her daughter
in her sprint around the track.
I am not the handgun
tossed into the weeds
of an abandoned lot
in the broken red brick
of this city I have passed through
with the remove
of a traveler;

I am not even that flap of blue tarpaulin,
that rooftop turbine,
there, dim silver crown
spinning over the city
for forty-five years.

*

It is before Duluth.
It is after Jerusalem. It is four
right hands held outward
as in the stone limbs of the lepers extending
toward the saint at the base of the shrine
at Saint Mary's. It is before Toledo.
It is after Sodom. It is the horror
zipped inside the yellow bag
fished from beneath
the bridge from the slate
water at the end of December,
it is the chemical dusk
coaled and burning out the day
over the tollbooths by Salina,
seventy-five cents dropped
into the perforated slot

to lift the arm of the gate,
and twenty dollars still can't save a life.

*

But I would not see the candle factory
washed of its salt stains, the open stars
of missing glass
smashed past
and swapped for lofts;
I have sworn to always return
to rest white flowers
on the back of moving water
among willows thick with summer
in the third week of September
to remember the one death
I carry through this city
like an interior
pin—
and the woman who bears it,
whom I love,
who was born here,
and I will not name.

*

What would the city say?

        (Whole worn corridors
               veiled
        in mechanical light)

The city doesn't speak,
it does not pray, it does not turn into memories of the dead
those two red beacons

blinking deeply into space,
its sky is not a sound
like intake, ancient whale breathing
against the ear of something small.

I would like to sit again
on the stone steps on
Trinity Place
offering whatever consolation I have left
to the dying man holding flowers
up to sunlight
in his last days on earth.
I gave him money
and listened to a story about his sister.
I should have held his hand.

Blue Handgun

All year I felt I was preparing for something.

A man passed me on the street
saying, *Something in your face*
makes me want to hurt you.

There was a spider on my bedroom wall—when I crushed it
something clicked.

I thought:
if it were bigger—
if it had left a greater mess.

Its legs
made a smeared trace
against the wall,
small.

The sound was them breaking.

*

When I was seven I watched a man crawl across the lawn
away from my father. No crowbar, no blood
that I remember—the scene is grey
except for the black fence
where we chained the black Labrador. Grey, and no blood,
but the man's face, it's twisted
as he crawls—what a dog's jaw might do
to a sneaker.

*

For nights after I'd killed it
I woke and shined a light
on what the spider's legs
had left.

      Bloodless, crusted—

by day I studied it—

      scentless, erasable—

the wishbone stain—

*

I went to bars. From the bathroom, I could hear the men
laughing in the other room.

I could smell the piss
in the warmth, the floors

black as the back of a beetle. I liked it, the smell

like the smell of the dirt floor
in my father's basement.

Down there,
saws had lined the walls.

There'd been a place for each,
an outline down to teeth
where the tool fit perfectly.

*

The street was Magnolia, and there'd been two men,
not one. One stood by the idling car
while a sound trickled
from the mouth
of his friend.

There were pale prints in the grass
where the man's hands and knees
had pressed,
lifted.

He crawled—
he rose—
he was choking—
he held a hand
around his throat.

*

What brought them back?
I couldn't say.

Spilled food—
bare wires

hanging
from the unlit
Citgo sign—

small things
frightened me.

My backpack knocked
a man's shoulder
on the subway—
he stared at me so long
I looked away.

I remembered Latin class,
the calendar of sunsets,
the disappointed teacher
reaching beneath his desk,

the blue handgun
my mind kept taped there.

*

I keep looking for the lesson.
My father is the tower.
I am only seven.
The lawn the long plain
leading to the castle.
The castle is the house.
The banisters are catapults.
The men, I know,
are meant to be extinguished.
I watch through my hands
as they approach.

*

What, in the end,
was done to me?

Nothing—

the men drove off,
the sun has bleached
the spider's stain,
my father cupped
the back of my head,
led me inside—

but something,

for I dream them
grown thinner, their prints
limping alone
across the lawn.

For weeks after,
through the bedroom window,
I could see them.

Who? my mother asked.
She didn't understand.

I meant the men. Every one is them.

III

After Psalm 17

I have no just cause
to plead you, Lord,
no violence to ask
you sully down
upon my enemy,
I have no enemy.
I have prayed, Lord,
and I have purposed,
I have purposed
that my mouth will
not transgress
but in psalm, Lord, in song
and silence, your name
rung from my tongue
is the hard rock
I knock upon
endlessly.
I have trusted, Lord.
I have disbelieved
and wanted, that my love
is built from you,
the blood of you, the world
you've built for me.
I worry, Lord. Have I knelt
not right nor enough?
Grace, god, light, white diamond
brightness, do I buttress
or beg not enough?
Bind, Lord, or find
me, paint me alone

and starve me, bully
or blind me with un-
curled, with unfurled
shadowed wings
that I may
my god
see at last
your likeness.
There has been no word
or sighting for many years.

A Story about the Moon

I'd been on this road before. Last year lit with wildflowers,
this year the hills stripped bare, baked by sun. It spills out
of Los Angeles like a long dark tongue, then nothing
for five hundred miles, just dust and shadows of cattle-sheds
past towns so small I turned off just to see who lives there.
My uncle in Oregon told me he got lost once, saw a sign
for a barn beside a creek beneath some pines: an hour
down the road he turned around. He liked the land, he said;
he bought it, never left. I think about that sometimes:
happenstance leading to a life; one set of faces replaced
by others. A girl I loved told me no one knows for certain
how the moon was formed. That there was earth
where now there are oceans, that a burning rock
slammed into us and the displaced land
became the moon. Back then she could toss a penny
from her bedroom and hit my window,
we lived that close. I remember one winter
passing the exit peeling off toward Cleveland.
She was living there with her father; by then we hardly spoke.
I thought—if I turned off, what would happen;
if I stopped? I think that's what I mean
about happenstance: where you are and how
you came to be there. And how cold the roads looked.
The ramp and the overpass and the thin metal
of the exit sign. How that day I just kept going.

Dispatch: Pittsburgh

It's 1770 or 1946 or 2018 in Iron City, Steel City,
   city of coal smoke and bridges, the tongue-twisting
     Monongahela
shifting the narrative: there was Indian dominion
over the upper Ohio Valley, Sawcunk and Logstown,
   outposts of the Iroquois and Shawnee. There was a vision
     and a battle, vicious
histories, the red oval of my mouth as I floated over tribal chiefs
receiving blankets from the Europeans, a scream
that no one heard.
   I sleep on couches and turn my body
to face the cushions and keep my shoes laced and gaping
on the floorboards below me, so when I wake
I step straight into daylight
in the city of five hundred bridges and cross number seventy-six
   into 1812
to watch the smokestacks and forges spring up on the flatlands,
  a city formed by warfare.
They called it the Westward Portal
until destiny manifested itself and it became the Smoky City,
   the Typhoid Capital, blooms forming
from the hot rolling of ingot stock, iron ore crushed
in the sinter plants, the deposits roiling the rivers to 130 degrees.
In divine time I stood with Carnegie
on the gilded balcony of his east side mansion: we toasted
Clinton and Soho, whose iron furnaces brought coke-fire
   smelting to the region.
   And I danced at the Battery Ball with Rockefeller's daughter:
   we cakewalked

into a two-step, polka'd into a waltz, and I left her
mid-mazurka to blitz the buffet table.
I came back in sixty-five years to find her a skeleton
frozen in a permanent twirl, her pearls glowing brightly in the
    ballroom lights,
and I lapped at the champagne still dripping from her rib cage.
    But there was no time to waste—
it was 1944, there was a war on—
so I snatched the pearls from her neck
and loaded them into my Colt Commando and marched out
into the Arsenal of Democracy.
    I high-stepped to the navy yards where tanned sailors leaned
out of the portholes while their girls knelt with bent necks—
it looked like praying—
and I cheered the men's departure
while their sisters wept into my shoulders,
and I jeweled the night sky
with my gunshots.
                    Then I walked across the Liberty Bridge
and felt the factories chip and crumble behind me,
and when I reached the other side it was 1973, my gun had rusted,
and I slid across beds of shattered glass chanting
    white flight, rust belt, brain drain, mercy, and knifed
into the bottom of a fountain where the Allegheny joins the
    Monongahela,
and I closed my eyes and slept for forty years.
When I woke I was surrounded by dimes and pennies, it was 2018,
    just another wartime Sunday, so I shrugged
and played the lotto and followed the streams of people to Heinz
    Field
where the Steelers lined up to play the Chiefs.
And I scalped tickets in the bright light of the winter parking lot;

and I told anyone who would listen they used to call this city
  Hell with the Lid Off;
and the crowds moved around me, I hovered above them,
and everyone wore yellow sweatshirts, and the arms
  were stitched with black hearts and stars.

Picasso in Milwaukee

I live where everything is bleached
pale by time and weather. I live outside
of where you watched the landscape peel
away at the edges and assumed that life lived on
beyond it. There was a painter whose eyesight failed
while his paintings grew brighter,
and brightly painted women hung
from canopies, slung
themselves over rows of gaping mouths.
Now the weeds have reclaimed the shoreline
and the river runs by itself.
If there's language anymore
it's a strange calligraphy
of bare trees. Collapsed
spinnakers float like water lilies,
and bodies in graves have turned
to earth; even the plants are broken
at the ankles. All along the boardwalk
the palisades guard emptiness; no one comes to visit me.
The smokestacks still feed the clouds
and sometimes there's a strange light
in the middle of the sky, a fiery rose
unfolding above me,
descending. I get scared
when I can barely
see the bridge.

Dispatch: Canal Zone
New York State, 1817–1825

And I heard the high F of the horn in the morning
and the steel of the swing as the axe blades placed
their notches, each tree dressed in chains
as the horses pushed forward
as the wheel turned
as the earth screamed beneath us
until the stumps sprang free.
And we came from Connemara, or we came from County
    Down
and Germany, we were ship-thin and picked by the dozen
and trafficked with the cattle
to the upstate Burned-Over ports.

This before the steam engine.
This before Camden and Amboy. This before King Class
    locomotives
drove the wilds west. This the time of diviners
and Seminole war, days the mule was beast, steaming,
    beaten, barge-puller, plow-
hound, bagged-up, roped, whip-flicked and grinning
beneath the weight of a one-ton load.

Summer one we opened earth at Rome.
Summer two our eardrums ruptured
from powder blasts and landslides, the muskets flashing
on our shoulders, Saturday brawls
fired by tiredness and whiskey.
Summer three and the forest burned: we prayed, we did not
    see angels

in the smoke shapes, we quit and came back and quit
and came back to the same thin wages, shanty-floor boredom
and each hour's lone parched cracked-lip suck of sun-sick
    whiskey. Our life
was the lock, the pier, the mud, the stop gate,
the culvert, the waste weir, the bridge spines
shining in the morning, and what was wilderness
became a "Westward Way," garrisoned
then townshipped then trade route and church-topped and
risen with a hand-stitched flag. Summer seven
we all fell sick from fever and dreams
of childhood thresholds or the wind off a coast
or just what sunlight looked like once
in the mornings in the skillets
in the kitchens of our homes.

And I was from Pittsburgh. Or I was from Aurora. Or I was
    born German
but the border took my name. And we won't be known as
    the Moseses
of history or gloried and canvassed in oil like DeWitt Clinton
pouring inland water into New York Harbor, but we are
    buried in Rome,
and we are buried at Scotia, we are buried at Troy
and Vischer Ferry, and once we carried the Erie up to
    Lockport,
drove it over Irondequoit Creek and spanned the Genesee:
a billion pounds of water
at our bidding, a billion pounds of rock clocked to nothing
at our powder. This before the days of gown and dowry,
this before the cannonade as the first boats left Buffalo,
when we were the lone souls north
beneath the porridge of the nighttime skies,

this before the railways,
when smoke meant the homestead, and north was the light
at the leftmost tip of the Dipper, and everyone died of malaria
and longing, and they closed our eyes with coins
bearing wreaths, clouds, years, flowing hair.

Salt Lake

Noon turned everything white—
   heat—
and empty—
    shadows walked back
inside their trees.

You were supposed to find God here,
the signs said—

West Jordan, Zion, there

where the first Saints
were fed
into the Valley
by the Range.

Dusk drowned the canyon's gashes—

dawn brought them back.

Then all that sunlight. All that

brown burnt trackside brush.
Kids by the roadside,
I remember—blue snow cones
in white paper cups.

Forbes Field, Pittsburgh, 1966

Anyone can tell it's hopeless: early July, jackhammer heat,
Pittsburgh down two in the tenth—even the diehards
in the bleachers are heading for the exits. Why shouldn't they?
It's late, work starts early, it's just another midsummer Sunday
     night game,
everyone dreading Monday morning, everyone dying of heat
in the grandstand's packed rows. So most are standing to leave
when a runner gets to first. And then another.
And so a hum starts up, and suddenly the pitcher
can't find the strike zone. And the fans edging to the exits
keep glancing back as a flutter like a wind
begins to rise: it's the crowd. It's the skin
on skin of clapping hands, it's whistles, it's the whine
of hinges as the kids in the nosebleeds stand
to see the batter slap a curveball to the gap in center.
A run scores, Bucs now down one. And the frenzy begins
when Roberto Clemente, muscle-car arms, soon-to-be MVP,
     steps to the plate
and sends a sinker a mile past left for the win.

I've heard the recording: mob scene, chaos, deep stampede, voices
like the roar of water falling into water. Think of it: fathers
unpocketing their Zippos, lighting last smokes, the kids
catcalling for Clemente to take another bow, only July but everyone
talking first place, Pennant race, World Series win, light
like benedictory oil all across the field. No one wants to go home.
And leaving through the gates, a young man in a banded trilby
stops to feel the heat of the assembled, the change in energy.
And seeing the packed trams—men piling up the steps,

skirted girls fleeced in street-lit gold—shrugs
and buys a pint of Flagstaff from the vendor at the exit
and begins the long walk back to his Allentown flat.

That man was my grandfather. He knows he won't get home
till well past midnight. And he'll tell this story to his son, my father,
who will pass it on to me, how he decided right then
to take tomorrow off work, take the paper to Roscoe's
for coffee, for grape jam spread thick on black toast,
for a seat in the sunlight in a booth by the window
where he'll sit all day and read about the win.
He'll tell how crossing home that night over Hot Metal's span,
he looked upriver to see the nighttime shine of the city's
    hundred bridges—
Tenth Street's towers, the tied arch of Birmingham
loping the Monongahela, Liberty's double-deck grillwork
lashing land to land like a rail tie, like a great animal spine
stretched across the water.

I like to think how the story must have swelled
in the coming months, as these stories do:
a minor embellishment
when he tells it to the waitress (*Clemente sent it 600 feet*),
a little something more when he tells it to a neighbor
(*the crowd was fifty thousand strong*), the story tricked into myth
by the time it finds the welders at Jones and Laughlin—the odds
    now impossible,
the heat like a steel mill, how the heart of the ball
tore off its cover in its flight across the wall.

But here are the facts: two weeks from that night
he'll meet my grandmother. By November they'll be married.

Pittsburgh will slip to third in the last week of the season
and lose out on the Pennant. Roberto Clemente will hit .317,
win the MVP, die young in December of '72
in a plane crash off coastal Puerto Rico.
And over the years, the details of that night
will not be so much lost
as evened out, bleached into other summers: somewhere
a heat wave, somewhere tall beers on a sun-hot bumper,
summer the Jones and Laughlin Steel Co. moved to South Side;
summer the fog flanked the river till it was known
only by its sound.

So when it reaches me from my grandfather's lips,
that July night in Forbes Field will have been whittled down
to its pinprick significance: no Gene Kelly glow, no nostalgia
       of firework light
from road flares cutting lanes through the postgame crowd,
just an old man's memory of heat and floodlights, a ball game
in summer, deep shadows on chessboard grass,
thin now as the tremor in his hand
as he points across the water and tells it
as he remembers: *It was midnight in July.*
I was just a young man. And I walked home over the bridge.

IV

The Leavings

Now there is no snow falling, no blue
November road we traveled,
    no bowlegged Saturday balcony
we sat on watching traffic pass,
    the traffic's gone.
No telegrams of smoke
twisting off the city's stacks, no river
of firefly headlights inching down
the distant hill, our chairs
abandoned, our glasses
drinking dust, toppled
by the wind—
    even the mailman's vanished,
though his cart remains, orange
in the porch light, leaves
like yellow letters
choking its open throat.

  *

Forgive me, darling,
I'm putting it all in—
    the bridge graffiti's prayer
for better seasons,
the red-brick perfect
    abandoned chapel we touched
our lips to
each time driving by it, the lines
like piano keys
    the light

through blinds placed
across your naked back—

    but the bottle,
too, the needle, our fingerprinted
      necks—
           and the worn
           jean jacket, moon-blue
denim ripped
    across the chest, mine
before it was yours: the thread,
    the stitches, the patch, the leavings—

   *

Can you see me?
    I'm that shadow
on a North Dakota road.
    I'm stuck in a dust storm
on a highway outside
    Casper,
    Idaho,
    Riley,
    Reno,
Bone. I'm tracing the places,
the unzipped
skin, the six-inch gashes
you laced across your ribs
    with the pyramid tip
        of a carpenter's nail.
I carry them with me.

   *

Goodbye!
Goodbye. The sky
    an indecision. The sky
a milky morning
    brightness, blinding.

The sky like the longest letter ever written
        never sent—
            I am trying to explain
how the road can be a bandage.

*

A black one. Unraveled. Tar-slicked
like the slashes
        of a Motherwell
abstract canvas.   When I last saw you

you were crying, you were
    small, the missing part
        of a chipped tooth, your image
diminishing
    in the rearview mirror—

in your summer dress and sandals,
standing in the center of the road.

Goodbye Friday street!
    Goodbye Syracuse,
cream-brick church top flocked
    with birds. Goodbye abandoned
china factory, famous
coffin maker, winter ribbon cinched
around my heart—

        goodbye
Jessica, daughter of blizzards,
        stone girl
splitting open—
            I am passing
                    the last madhouse
            outskirt smokestack,

I am crying.

*

You kept the rain jar.

I kept the thrift store divinity medal,
        the '67 penny
in the heel of my sneaker.

You kept the dead yellow flowers
        wrapped in a road map, a bottle cap
of sleeping bees. I kept the single

moth wing sealed
        in its envelope, your name
across the cover.

You kept the jacket,
        I the missing button, silver tarnished mark
I carry always in my pocket.

*

Tonight I walk out into stars,
the everyday shotgun
stars, dumb knucklebone

burnings, scattershot, trapped
in the moon's blue corona.

The horizon's on fire.

I know it is only the light
from port cranes, their night-lit
tips, but I imagine a factory in flames
beneath it, withered back to its frame.

Once, from the front porch, in the snow,
I screamed your name
so loudly into darkness
I woke the neighbors. You turned back
to look at me. In your torn
jean jacket. Saturday at 3:00 a.m.
Years ago. The crooked patch we sewed.
The crazy white stitching.

Calaveras

February, grapevines
spare as crosses—

driving east across the valley, strict
rows of flowering almonds,
a blossom carpet
underneath
I first mistook for snow.

I first mistook Copperopolis
for Angels Camp. I thought Murphys was Dorrington.
When I was a child, I'd lie so still
I believed I could feel the earth
hurling me as it turned.

Up above the snow line,
ash flickers from a brush pile
burning at the shore—

the lake face frozen—

bare aspens stiff
against the sky.

I lie down on stone.
I lie down sideways
so the tree line makes a gash
between the ice and sky—

white fir. Blue ice. Dark imprint
of a child dragging a sled
across the lake.

The world when it slows enough for me to see—

child on ice,
black aspens,
white sky

Bands You Might Have Liked If You Were Still Alive
For M. G.

Pantera, little king. Danzig's *Lucifuge*, Black Sabbath or Alice
    in Chains, something with bite marks
and metal on the wrist. Because you laughed from the brain-
swell of nitrous oxide huffed from a punch-balloon's flute.
    Because you were a bastard. Because you were brick
    to window, window to the undone
glass along the pavement, a surprise in the softness
    of your *Sorry*.

Wilco for Chicago, *Yankee Hotel Foxtrot*, temple
    hymnal for the Sabbath you swapped
the juice for wine and went red as a Testament robe.
Something Rome for a city
    you never went to, something requiem
because your parents died before you.

Lou Reed, little prince, Patricia Lee, Iggy
    Pop's "Passenger" you were too young
to know. Dodos for the sixth song's solo alone:
the string sounds, the shout, the jungle drums
    coming back in: like flight, Michael, like light
to the lakeside sky we were drunk, shrug, dumb enough to
    leap beneath
from cliff ledge to glass-flat dawn-dulled water. Our splay
    to pale knives falling to that blackness. Phoenix
because you are ash.

Wavves, Sun Kil, The Walkmen's sun-washed *Lisbon*, because
you would forgive, Michael, these words, my sentimental
    and all-night
drinking among friends who remember you,
    better, loved you
with a rage like blindness, the sun against an eye.
Because I still don't know
    if you meant to leave us.

Something commissioned, little king. Something Philly, finally,
as that's how I remember you best: still with your kid-fat,
    your Little League tee,
our hands together on the spool: November
and letting it out, the kite's slow rise, the crows flying by us:
    how you just
took over, walked off, left me at the park edge, followed that
    high stitch deep
into the field—

Stopping the War

The most I ever did to stop it
was walk through Chicago carrying a comet
on a piece of cardboard.

It was winter; our grim procession flowed
through the frozen city.
And under the spark and arc

of the comet's flaking tail
was Nelson Mandela's face,
digitally shifted

so tears streamed from his cheekbones
in the colors of the flag.

Is it possible I wanted peace?
I was sixteen—joysticked missiles
flashed greenly
into Baghdad.

I kept the sign
because I liked the comet.
I stayed up late
watching night-vision raids.
I wanted us to win.

*

More than lying to our parents,
more than Saturday nights
in the lot behind Allied

doing moon-bounds
down the lengths of metal sheeting,
better than tequila and Spanish Audrey

pulling me toward her
downward
onto her older sister's foldout bed,

were Fridays, 3:00 p.m.,
Ian, me, and Ryan
in the Demon Dog parking lot,

soft-pack Parliaments
and a half pint of Seagram's on the dash.
I liked how Ryan drove—fast,

but I trusted it,
like the car was a part of him—
I liked how he'd be halfway through the Seagram's
while me and Ian
still had a half period left of Geometry.

We'd eat Polishes in the parking lot
with our backpacks stashed in his car.
We'd watch the sparks shatter
from the tracks of the Elevated
each time the Red Line
screamed past.

*

At the dinner table
my mother passed out pins

with the image of a gas-masked soldier
locked behind a peace sign—

in room 402
I was put on trial for war crimes
in Rwanda
in a history class imagined
as the Tanzanian courtroom
used in 1995
for the UN tribunal
on genocide—

Sundays I walked the path past
Belmont Harbor
to the stone atrium
overlooking the lake.

Geese screamed. Crushed cans
drifted by the inlet.
I came for the way the line

between water and sky just
collapsed as the light fell to one
pale wall of pewter and blue;

to see the beacons glow red
on the stone shoulders
of the grey intake tower standing
like a stanchion in the deep.

*

There's a poem where the protesters know each other
by their missing little fingers, sawed off in dissent
and mailed to the president.

I like that thought: hoses, marches, leashes and teeth,
ten thousand pinkies piled on a desk—

then years later, two strangers
meeting in Michigan or Warsaw
or the fog of a lakeside park: pine in winter,

hand on a bench-back, hand brushing back
a strand of hair: no wars for forty years.
Two ex-dissidents flashing their gaps in recognition.

*

Late spring we won State.
On television, tanks
with chain-wrapped wheels

under giant crossing sabers
in Grand Festivities Square,
Baghdad.

At home I clicked through pictures
of those 1960s Saigon monks—bone thin
in sunlight, in saffron
robes, in the center of an intersection,
their friends pouring petrol on their heads

before the men pressed their foreheads to the pavement,
then struck and touched their bodies with a match.

The swirling shapes of flame
around their torsos made me think
how ice cream twists from a machine

into a waiting cone.
They pinned their robes so closely
they became impossible to save.

*

And they didn't want saving,
they wanted to make a point,

like my mother, in 1968,
lacing seventy-five nails
through a tennis ball

and placing it
beneath a cop car's
front wheel.

Khe Sanh. Kent State. Daley
in the mayor's hall. She had chopped black hair
and plain white sneakers.

Ninh Binh. Blue water
and bombers coming off the shore.
My mother kneeling beside the wheel. *Bang*
when it rolled.

*

You can go to war and come back
missing half a face.
You can send a drone to Pakistan

and open up the insides of a hospital
full of children. You might return alive
but with a stripe of filmstrip in your brain

shining with something living
while it burns.

Nevertheless, when Ryan enlisted I was excited.
A friend in the army. I liked how it sounded.
I liked the world I pictured it building

in the mind of anyone I'd tell—gunfire and winter,
childhoods of trash can barbecues,
fake metal of a Remington replica swapped

for the grip and raised block script
of a handgun
hanging easy from a muscled waist,
some imagined toughness reflected back to me.

I shaved my head.
He went through basic.
I went to college.
He landed in Afghanistan.
I carried a duffel,
I let a woman in an airport shake my hand
and thank me for my service.

*

Some days I ride the El
all evening through Chicago's downtown
loop, past the campuses and stone

lions and libraries and fireproofed brick-
backed dominions where inside
the business of the city

spins like a turnstile. There's the fountain
where kids toss pennies
for a wish. There's the convention center

where the Democrats gathered in 1968.
There's the park where my mother was billy-clubbed
and teargassed with the rest of them.

There's that strip
off the Kennedy Expressway
which meant nothing

until I read that activist
Malachi Ritscher burned himself to death in protest,
circa November 2006.

To which the newspapers said,
"With all great respect,
his last gesture on this planet
was his saddest, and most futile."

*

How does a war end? With airlifts and crowds
amassing at the gate; elsewhere soldiers
stripping gear from their shoulders and diving
headlong   star-splayed   Geronimo   down
into Ha Long Bay. With a banner

on an airship claiming victory,
the war still going. In Buffalo,
Gary, south Chicago, with kids

doing benzos in the alley
outside the strip mall; in emerald green
on the day of the parade;

with the outline of Illinois
tattooed on Ryan's bicep
the summer he came back, a red star

inked inside the center of the state.

*

Honor to the writers of the Great Manifestos,
the pens of the addled visionaries
scribbling missives for peace.

Honor to my mother,
who fights for the long arc, believing it bends
toward justice.

Honor to Ryan, who knows the patterns
cast on a sandstone wall
when the head of a leaping dog
opens for a bullet—

I am thankful he came back.

And honor to Chicago, the steel blue
of the lake one winter afternoon
glimpsed from the window of a train—

where I angled my cardboard Mandela
so everyone could see what I stood for;
where outside

the city passed in a scramble
of ductwork and water-holds
and rusted metal mushroom turbines

turning with the wind;
and a vacant lot
where someone had spray-painted a bomber

inside a giant circle: red wings, black tail
spread to the circle's edge,
making the sign for peace.

Which I looked at. Which I put here
because I thought it pretty,
and because it felt significant,
and because I remember.

Rainout in the Twin Cities

On the radio, the announcers
narrate the day's scores. I can hear the pink mist
drift up, fold and unfold
around the night-lit skyscrapers.
The grounds crew unrolls the blue tarp,
the players store their gloves,
untie their shoes. I am alone.
This is the hour the dishes knock
against their brothers, the only child
opens the cold white room
to peer in. Outside, two raccoons
pause crossing the street. Their lightness.
The lightness of a neighbor's moan
carrying through the air,
like a touch. I crush
the last cigarette into the heel
of my sneaker. The train horn. The blanket
of pink clouds. They're the same sound. The click
as the lit room goes dark.

Memorial Day

I was on the porch deck
gluing strips of cut-up newspaper
to a sheet of flattened cardboard
across from the apartment
where for one sticky summer
I slept with a college girl
who painted and drank beer through straws
and told me how she used to cry alone
on the cold pavement of her parents' darkened garage.
I was making plans for the next seventy years.
    On the street everyone was playing a game called bags—
stitched silk bean sacks tossed through holes in plywood
        boards—
and the city seemed quiet, everyone buying charcoal
and listening to the radio where the news was bone-sad
as anyone could bear: high-rises clouding the sky above Mecca,
a woman beneath them begging from her knees,
        two black holes
where her eyes used to be; a vet in Toledo rolling his chair
to a lakeside hot dog stand, motorboats and laughter.
    All along the street the bars were shifting servers
and it was night: I spread out in the bathtub
like some mythic winter king, though really I was scared
and ashamed and thinking
even thunder can sound like longing,
moving through the sky, trying to find its place—
        and outside, fires
were lit in every city backyard,
the ice had melted, the radios were quiet,

my eyes were closing, the oil was burning, my hands were
    soaking, the cars were turning
five hundred miles on an Indiana speedway—

Mother Marys, steel engines, greasy hearts

Acknowledgments

I would like to thank the editors of the following journals in which some of these poems first appeared, sometimes in slightly different versions: *Adroit Journal*; *Coffin Factory*; *Cortland Review*; *Diode Poetry Journal*; *Forklift, Ohio*; *Iowa Review Online*; *Midwestern Gothic*; *Nashville Review*; *Ninth Letter*; *Superstition Review*; and *Tinderbox Poetry Journal*.

Grateful acknowledgment is also made to Patrick Riedy and PressBoardPress, who published my 2015 chapbook, *the sky is not cotton*, which included versions of "Explaining the Resurrection in Simple Words," "Syracuse, October," and "The Life."

Some of the poems in this collection were written during my time at Syracuse University and while at Stanford University as a Wallace Stegner Fellow. I am deeply indebted to the poets that I have been so lucky to learn from at each place: Eavan Boland, Michael Burkard, Ken Fields, Louise Glück, Sarah Harwell, Brooks Haxton, Mary Karr, Chris Kennedy, and Bruce Smith. And to Gabrielle Calvocoressi and David Means—thank you for your writing and your support.

I am particularly grateful to Louise Glück—for your writing, friendship, enormous generosity, and invaluable help in shaping these poems and this book—and to Bruce Smith and Michael Burkard, for your friendship and the inspiration of your own work. You are each a guiding light to me.

Thanks, especially, to Henri Cole, for selecting this book and for your guidance and advice in helping me turn it from a shifting draft-stage manuscript into something final and improved.

I am very fortunate to be joining Milkweed Editions and the roster of talented writers they support. Thanks to everyone there for your help in beautifully realizing this book. I am lucky to get to work with you.

This would not be possible without the life and writing of Max Ritvo. I am grateful to Max's family—particularly Ariella Ritvo-Slifka and the Alan B. Slifka Foundation—for collaborating with Milkweed to make this prize possible. I only hope that I can carry something of Max's loving and generous spirit forward.

So many were a part of this book. Thanks to the community of folks I studied with at Syracuse (particularly Adam, Chen, Tim, Becca, and Jess), Stanford, the NY State Summer Writers Institute, and the Norman Mailer Center. For your steadfast friendship, your writing and your insight, I thank Adam Bright, Tim Craven, Noah Warren, Edgar Kunz, Laura Romeyn, Margaret Ross, Will Brewer, Brian Tierney, Casey Thayer, Eric Berlin, and Jessica Scicchitano.

Most of all, thank you to my parents and my sister, for your love and support always and in all things, and to Jessica, whose stamp goes far beyond the words, and who I am lucky to share this with: to our morning views through the windows of many different kitchens, and to many more.

Jessica Scicchitano

Grady Chambers was born and raised in Chicago. He was a Wallace Stegner Fellow at Stanford University, attended the MFA program at Syracuse University, and has received fellowships from the Norman Mailer Center and the New York State Summer Writers Institute. His writing has appeared in *Adroit Journal*; *Diode Poetry Journal*; *Forklift, Ohio*; *Nashville Review*; *New Ohio Review*; *Ninth Letter*; and elsewhere. He lives in Philadelphia.

The inaugural award of the

MAX RITVO POETRY PRIZE

is presented to

GRADY CHAMBERS

by

MILKWEED EDITIONS
and
THE ALAN B. SLIFKA FOUNDATION

Designed to honor the legacy of one of the most original
poets to debut in recent years—and to reward outstanding
poets for years to come—the Max Ritvo Poetry Prize
awards $10,000 and publication by Milkweed Editions to
the author of a debut collection of poems. The 2017 Max
Ritvo Poetry Prize was judged by Henri Cole.

Milkweed Editions thanks the Alan B. Slifka Foundation
and its president, Riva Ariella Ritvo-Slifka, for supporting
the Max Ritvo Poetry Prize.

milkweed
editions

Founded as a nonprofit organization in 1980,
Milkweed Editions is an independent publisher.
Our mission is to identify, nurture and publish
transformative literature, and build an engaged
community around it.

Milkweed Editions is based in Bdé Óta Othúŋwe
(Minneapolis) within Mní Sota Makhóčhe, the traditional
homeland of the Dakhóta people. Residing here since time
immemorial, Dakhóta people still call Mní Sota Makhóčhe
home, with four federally recognized Dakhóta nations and
many more Dakhóta people residing in what is now the state
of Minnesota. Due to continued legacies of colonization,
genocide, and forced removal, generations of Dakhóta
people remain disenfranchised from their traditional
homeland. Presently, Mní Sota Makhóčhe has become a
refuge and home for many Indigenous nations and peoples,
including seven federally recognized Ojibwe nations. We
humbly encourage our readers to reflect upon the historical
legacies held in the lands they occupy.

milkweed.org

Interior design by Mary Austin Speaker
Typeset in Caslon

Adobe Caslon Pro was created by Carol Twombly
for Adobe Systems in 1990. Her design was inspired by
the family of typefaces cut by the celebrated engraver
William Caslon I, whose family foundry served
England with clean, elegant type from the early
Enlightenment through the turn
of the twentieth century.